TOTALLY INFATUATED

PURSUING A LIFE-CHANGING
PASSION FOR GOD'S WORD

JACQUELINE PIERRE

FOREWORD BY KURT JOHNSTON

simply for students

Totally Infatuated: Pursuing a Life-Changing Passion for God's Word

group.com
simplyyouthministry.com

Credits

Author: Jacqueline Pierre

Executive Developer: Nadim Najm

Chief Creative Officer: Joani Schultz

Editor: Rob Cunningham

Art Director: Veronica Lucas

Production Manager: DeAnne Lear

ISBN 978-0-7644-8192-5

10 9 8 7 6 5 4 3 2   20 19 18 17 16 15 14 13 12

Printed in the United States of America.

DEDICATION

I dedicate this book, first and foremost,
to my Lord and Savior, Jesus Christ,
who paid the price for my sin on the cross
and gave me his precious words
to guide and direct me through this crazy life.

And to the four most infatuated people I know: my family.

To my Dad and Mom for loving me,
for showing me what it means to be infatuated with God's Word,
for modeling service in the church in front of me,
and for creating a happy home for me, my entire life.

To my brother, Robert, for his sacrificial support,
the godly example he sets for me to follow,
and for his signature rambunctious love he has freely offered this
little sister.

And to "Mom" for her generous love, her rock solid counsel,
and her wealth of knowledge, especially biblical,
that I have been privileged to sit under, as her granddaughter.

I love you guys with all my heart.

*I will never forget the night Billy Graham spoke this earthquaking statement in my presence! He said, "The world has yet to see what God can do with one human life, completely yielded and sold out to him!" Now after reading Jacqueline Pierre's awe-inspiring Totally Infatuated, I'm convinced she's well on her way to shaking the youth of our nation! Starting at chapter 1, and **never stopping** till the last word of chapter 11, I was overwhelmed, overjoyed, and totally infatuated! JP's young ability to inspire the "whole of me" blessed me as much as any evangelist's message to the masses. I am proud to call her "lil sis," but most of all, a female David—a world changer!*

–Michael Tait

Grammy® Award-Winning Recording Artist, Newsboys and DC Talk

Confession: I am infatuated with JP and her vision! First an adorable, infectious little girl, then a fierce competitor through junior high. Now a beautiful young woman directing her God-given passion into others finding what she discovered in God's Word! Listen to her. Learn from her and love what she loves. Follow her advice in Totally Infatuated and your life will sparkle with the glory of God as hers does!

–James MacDonald

Senior Pastor, Harvest Bible Chapel
Walk in the Word Broadcast Ministries

This book is like Red Bull® for your Bible desire! It's full-on, solid, serious, no-playing, standing up for God's Word! True to the bone, heart and passion about the Bible being the call maker on all decisions in life! Jacqueline puts the Bible back in its rightful place, in front of our eyes and hidden in our hearts!

–Tony Nolan
Author and Speaker

As a pastor and dad of junior high students, I'm grateful for the message God has given Jacqueline. It's great substance made clear and simple—taking on the fundamentals of what it means to practically and thoughtfully live the Christ-life. She ups the ante for the reader ready to get serious about the substance of God's Word and its inherent purpose to infect belief and behavior. God's Word, a genuine walk with Christ, friends, identity issues…all here…so buckle up and read!

–Joel Anderson
Senior Pastor, Harvest Bible Chapel Orlando

This is a great book that any teenager could relate to. Jacqueline approaches every adolescent's main struggle—identity. She does this by relating to her peers, and with an honest desire to speak truth to their hearts. A must-read for any teen that feels like there's more than this world has to offer.

–Jeff Owen
Recording Artist, Tenth Avenue North

If the Bible has made no real impact on your life, I challenge you to listen to a 15-year-old who's been rocked by its message in ways that would surprise you. Every student in America needs to read this book!

-Johnny Scott
Christ In Youth

Jacqueline Pierre's Totally Infatuated is something you rarely find these days, a book with honesty, passion, and heart. She writes in a way that truly captures the spirit of a young adult trying to change the world for Christ. Courageous and convicting at times and lovingly affectionate at others, Totally Infatuated is a sincere prayer to help us all understand life's journey by keeping the Word of God close to our heart. Pierre's passion for the Bible runs deep, and after reading this book, when it comes to the Word of God, "I trust that you, too, will become totally infatuated."

-Dave Frey
Recording Artist, Sidewalk Prophets

INFATUATED:

To have an all-absorbing passion.

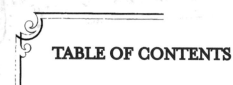

TABLE OF CONTENTS

FOREWORD

I'm not a teenager. But I'm the parent of two teenagers, and in my role as a youth pastor I have spent the last 25 years hanging out with teenagers just like you. And I have a confession to make: I think you happen to be the COOLEST people on the planet! That's why when Jacqueline asked me to write a brief foreword for this book, I was thrilled to do so.

When I first read the title—*Totally Infatuated*—I wasn't sure what this book might be about. After all, teenage girls like Jacqueline could be "totally infatuated" with just about anything, and I was a little nervous about what I might read in these pages.

So it would be fair to say I was shocked—and thrilled—to discover that this book is all about the Bible!

I don't know exactly how much time the average teenage follower of Jesus spends reading his/her Bible each week, but I'm pretty sure of this: It's not much. And because most teenagers don't do much Bible reading, they don't know much about it and how it relates to the world they find themselves navigating. One of my youth pastor friends recently had an experience that illustrates this. She decided to do a brief survey of the high schoolers in her youth group to test their Bible knowledge. To her dismay, 87 percent of the students couldn't even name all four Gospels! (Matthew, Mark, Luke, and John...in case you were wondering!) These weren't unchurched teenagers, or students who were brand-new to the faith; they had been around a while, and most of them considered themselves Christians.

Most teenagers simply don't read their Bible. And that's why I love any book about the Bible that is written for teenagers, especially one like this that is written for teenagers by a teenager! (Wow, how many times can I say "teenager" in this paragraph?)

In this book you will experience three things, and my prayer for you is that one or two of them will grab your attention and make you want to explore God's Word a little more often on your own.

First, you will read some compelling historical facts about the Bible: where it came from, the sacrifices made for us to have our own copies, and a bunch of other stuff. CRAZY stuff!

Second, as you read you will "hear" Jacqueline's enthusiasm and infatuation for God's Word.

Third, you will see how the Bible clearly speaks to some typical teenage issues—things you may be wrestling with or things that have left you wondering where to find answers.

A book like *Totally Infatuated* should never be read as a replacement for the Bible. Instead, books like this are meant to serve as a sort of springboard or launching pad to a lifetime of reading God's Word. But be warned: When you start spending time reading and exploring the Bible, you—just like Jacqueline has seen in her life—will become totally infatuated with it!

Praying for you,

Kurt Johnston
Youth Pastor, Saddleback Church

CHAPTER ONE

TOTALLY INFATUATED

Before I was even born, my grandfather began collecting old Bibles—really, really old Bibles. You may think that sounds pretty dusty and boring, but it might not after you hear the story that started it all. You see, back in the 1500s, England was ruled by a ruthless queen named Mary. Well, Mary decided to make a law that you could not own a Bible that was written in English. In fact, anyone who possessed a Bible that was written in English would be killed—found, captured, and dragged out into a public place, and their flesh set on fire. I can't even imagine it! Despite all that, some amazing people were so infatuated with the Word of God that they would do ANYTHING to keep it—even sacrifice their lives. So Mary killed many, many people in this way: men, women, and even children. This is how the queen earned the name "Bloody Mary."

As these people were burning at the stake and their bodies began to bleed, the soldiers were commanded to take each person's Bible, dip it into the puddle of blood, hold it up to show the horrified crowds, and then hurl it into the fire to burn, as well. Heavy stuff, right? Well, here's where the story get's good. See, my grandfather happened upon an English Bible from one of those events. Imagine that! A 500-year-old Bible. (That's more than twice as old as the United States!) A Bible that, amazingly, had been rescued before it burned along with its owner. But even though it survived, it still bore the scars from being at that scene of death: Each and every page was stained brick red from being dipped in the blood of the one who died for it. A powerful reminder of the passionate sacrifice of some unidentified owner!

I hate to take a break from this amazing story right now, but I have to think that you are wondering the same thing I wondered when I first heard this story: "What is it about this book that makes people so totally infatuated with it?" Well, the Bible is such an incredible treasure because it contains the very words of God, in written form, so you and I can understand God and God's will for us.

God—the almighty creator of the universe, all-powerful, all-knowing—has sent us a written letter!

Now, I know most of us don't get too many letters in the mail these days, but if you would allow me to use a somewhat lame illustration, it's kind of like getting a text. Can you imagine that? What if God sent you a text? Would you read it? (Bzzzzzzzz. Oh, it's a text from God himself.) Yeah, of course you would read it! Well, God HAS sent you a text—maybe not one on your cell phone, but one that was meant for you, carefully written down in the Bible.

The next question you may ask is, "How do you know? How do you know the Bible contains the very words of God?" Another great question! Just because I believe that the Bible is filled with God's words (or just because your mom or your dad or your pastor believes that) doesn't make it true. Tons of people believe in the tooth fairy, but that doesn't make her real. However, the thing about the Bible is that it can totally stand, no matter how or by whom it is evaluated.

For centuries, people have studied the facts and accuracy of the Bible, to see if they hold up as true. And guess what? Every word in the Bible has been proven true and reliable, whether it's a statement related to science or history or medicine.

Archaeology supports the facts of Scripture:
- Belshazzar, last king of Babylon
- Cuneiform dating pre-Moses, proving written language before Moses
- Stone monuments with the name of King David
- The Hittites
- Inscription with Pilate's name

5

> *"In all the writings of Buddha, Confucius, and Lao-tse, you will not find a single example of predicted prophecy. In the Koran (the writings of Muhammed) there is only one instance of a specific prophecy—a self-fulfilling prophecy—that he, Muhammed himself, would return to Mecca. Quite different from the prophesy of Jesus who said that He would return from the grave. One is easily fulfilled, and the other is impossible to any human being...The prophesies of Scripture, on the other hand, are incredibly specific and detailed. In the Old Testament alone there are two thousand predictive prophesies, not a few lucky guesses."* D. James Kennedy

In fact, there is more historical and archaeological evidence for the Word of God than any other book known to man! And if that's not enough, the Bible has predicted hundreds of things that have all come to happen, right to the smallest detail—in some cases, up to thousands of years ahead of time. Only God can do that!

So, going back to our opening story, there my grandfather sat looking at this blood-stained Bible and thinking about, for the first time, people dying for the right to have a Bible they could read. Dying for it! This kind of passion inspired him, and he began to collect very old, rare Bibles from all over the world, each one with a unique story about an owner—many who gave their whole life to protect or pass on the Bible. It is now one of the largest collections in private hands. (Oh, and by the way, it includes that blood-stained Bible.)

This is the link to the VanKampen Collection if you want to check it out:
solagroup.org/vkc.html

All this is very cool, but there is still one question out there. We know WHAT the Bible is. We know HOW it is the very Word of God. But the last question is, "WHY? Why did God bother to communicate to us?" The answer is because God loves us, he wants us to know him, and he wants to give us hope (see Romans 15:4-5). And because God loves us, we can love him, and we want to know what he has to say to us. Even though the Bible was written a long time ago, God's words do not become outdated. God's words are not like our cell phones and computers that become ridiculously obsolete every five years! And God's words have so much power that anyone who reads them and responds to them is never the same—they become a different person. They become totally infatuated with God's words. Whether that reader lived in the year 500, the year 1000, or here in the 21st century!

My name is Jacqueline Pierre, and I'm one of those people. I happily join the ranks of some of the greatest men and women in history who have loved the Word of God—people like John Wycliffe, John Hus, Martin Luther, William Tyndale, and John Calvin, just to name a few. Another was King David. In Psalm 119, he tells God about his love 11 times!

Here are a few of those verses:

..for I find my delight in your commandments, which I love (verse 47)
Therefore I love your commandments above gold, above fine gold (verse 127)
Consider how I love your precepts (verse 159).
My soul keeps your testimonies; I love them exceedingly (verse 167).

Love is a very serious thing. Have you ever become completely infatuated with someone? They say "falling in love" only takes 1/5th of a second[1] and is as strong as an addiction to cocaine[2], because falling in love affects the intellectual areas of the brain and triggers the same sensation of euphoria experienced by people when they take that drug. Now that's crazy! Effects of love include dilated eyes, weight loss, numb tongue, obsessive-compulsive behavior, clammy hands, sleeplessness, and, of course, butterflies in your stomach. A love like this is all-consuming; you want to know everything the object of your affection says and thinks, and you would give up everything for this person. This kind of passion is a very serious thing, and we think nothing of it when directed toward another person.

But what I propose is that you become infatuated with God. I mean it! Sold out. Totally obsessed. And when you do, you will be crazy about what God has to say to you in the letter written for you, his very words, the Bible—just like the people I described to you earlier, who were so crazy about the Bible that they gave their lives for it. Listen, I'm sure they didn't start out like that; they didn't become Christians and then suddenly have this urge to die for the Word of God. No, it probably didn't happen like that at all. If I had to guess, it probably happened like this: After they became Christians, they were so crazy in love with Jesus that they wanted to know what he had to say to them. So they began to read the Bible.

It probably didn't take them too long to really understand that the book they held in their hands gave guidance to their lives, and when they discovered this truth, their love for God's Word grew until they became totally infatuated with it—and decided that the words in their Bible were more valuable than anything else they could ever own.

The words of the Bible still are valuable today. That's how the obsession developed in me. Because I'm in love with Jesus, I'm crazy about the Bible. It is truth and it is relevant to the life I live here and now. I know that if you begin to read it, it will open your heart to God and change your life. It will bring you peace and success. Don't just take my word for it; I'll prove it to you. In the upcoming chapters I'm going to talk about how the Word of God speaks to some things we deal with every day—at home, at school, in private, and with friends. I hope you are amazed to find out how the Bible can be so current even though it's so "old." It's as alive and active today as it was a thousand years ago—you'll see. Stick with me! My prayer is that you'll fall in love with it, too. And soon, like me and the many people who have lived before, you will become totally infatuated with the Word of God.

CHAPTER TWO

WHO AM I?

Do you have a big brother? I do, and despite our occasional wrestle-to-the-ground, kicking-and-screaming, all-out battles, I think he's a pretty amazing kid. His name is Robert Pierre, and he's a Christian recording artist. He's such a humble guy; if you met him, you might not realize how much he has accomplished. But Robert has had the unique opportunity to sing for God and be an encouragement to hundreds of thousands of people all over the country.

Robert started touring when he was 13 years old, and when you ask him about that, he has some great stories about what it's like to live on a tour bus, perform while you have the stomach flu, sleep in a bunk the size of a coffin, and play basketball with  his tour-mates between gigs. But more than any of that, what's made the biggest impression on Robert has been meeting so many kids. Even though he's talked to thousands and thousands of them, each one is unique.

Each person has a special look, sound, talent, and interest. They've been from all across the country, from North Carolina all the way to Seattle, and they have been as different from one another as the football captain is from the geography bee champ!

But, interestingly enough, there is one way in which many of them are exactly the same. As Robert has gone from city to city, he's noticed that many teenagers don't know what they are here for, who they really are, or what makes them important. So many students are hurting, and they're trying to be loved or popular by becoming the things that the world says will get them noticed or make them happy: a superstar athlete, a magazine cover lookalike, a straight-A student, or something similar. Many have tried and failed. Some have succeeded but then found out that it didn't make them happy in the end. Teenagers in our generation are having an identity crisis!

Robert decided that today's teenagers needed to hear a much different message, and he began to write his second album, titled *Identity*. The message of this whole album is that our identity—who we are and what makes us important—cannot be found in anything that we are or anything that we do, but it has to be only in who Christ is and what he has done for us on the cross.

Nothing else!

Scripture says this:

> ³For we ourselves were once foolish, disobedient, led astray, slaves to various passions and pleasures, passing our days in malice and envy, hated by others and hating one another. ⁴But when the goodness and loving kindness of God our Savior appeared, ⁵he saved us, not because of works done by us in righteousness, but according to his own mercy, by the washing of regeneration and renewal of the Holy Spirit, ⁶whom he poured out on us richly through Jesus Christ our Savior... (Titus 3:3-6).

When God looks down at us, he can only see our sin. No matter how many great things we have done, if we have done just one sin, we deserve to be forever separated from God. His holiness cannot tolerate anything less than perfection. An undefeated season, straight-off-the-runway good looks, or a perfect SAT score won't impress God if you have committed even the slightest sin—and if you haven't guessed already, that means everyone's in the same boat: guilty.

But amazingly, there is hope! That hope comes through Jesus Christ, who is God himself and who put on flesh and became a man. Jesus, unlike anyone else who has ever lived, was totally without sin (see Hebrews 4:15). His brutal death on the cross served as a payment to cover our sins. This means that now, when looking down on those of us who have received this gift of salvation through Jesus, God the Father sees Christ's perfect, sinless blood covering all of our flaws and imperfections, and we are acceptable to God.

I have been crucified with Christ. It is no longer I who live, but Christ who lives in me. And the life I now live in the flesh I live by faith in the Son of God, who loved me and gave himself for me (Galatians 2:20).

At the point that you turn to God in repentance for your sin and believe that Jesus Christ is Savior and Lord, the Bible says you are saved (see Romans 10:9-10). We can receive forgiveness because of what Christ has already done, not by anything we do! Your identity is now found in Christ. You are a child of God and God's own possession (see 1 Peter 2:9-10). The world will tell you the polar opposite: that your identity should be all wrapped up in who YOU are. But that's all a lie, and if you believe it, you've been deceived. Christ says our self-worth must come from being a child of the creator of the universe. God says we are important and valued because we are a fellow heir with Christ (see Romans 8:17).

God says that our inner beauty is what is important, not our outward appearance. At the end of the day, it doesn't matter what the world thinks of you; it only matters what God thinks of you. When you truly understand that, it will change the way you live your life! You won't have to find your identity or significance by looking like that girl in the magazine, being the best player on the basketball team, or "going out with" (whatever that means) the cutest person at your school. You only have to look to Jesus for your hope and identity. Life is filled with constant change, but we serve an unchanging God. In the future, friends and even family may fail you, but Jesus Christ will never fail you.

So who are you? Are you someone who has found your identity in Christ, or are you someone whose identity is in crisis?

"That's who I am, forgiven and set free.
It doesn't matter what the world may think of me.
I got nothing to hide. I know my Identity.
Without a doubt I know His blood has covered me,
and THAT'S who I am."

Robert Pierre
Lyrics from the song "Identity"

robertpierre.com

CHAPTER THREE

THE BATTLE

I don't know about you, but I stink at math. I always have. Sure, I can pass the tests—but just barely! It's a lot of work for me, and even then, I'm just average. But to some of my friends, math is a breeze. It's as natural as tying their shoes. Ugh! So frustrating! Sometimes, when I've been working on my math homework for a couple of hours, this strange sensation comes over me: My mind tells me that all the answers to the homework are in the back of the book, right? So why not just copy them down? I mean, it's not like I haven't put the time in. I've been working for two hours already. What would be wrong with that? And so I think about that for a moment, until I'm reminded that it is CHEATING—and I choose to carry on with that stinkin'

Cheating statistics*
- Cheating typically begins in middle school
- Nine out of 10 middle schoolers admit to copying someone else's homework; two-thirds say they have cheated on exams
- Cheating most often occurs in science and math classes
- 75 percent to 98 percent of college students surveyed each year admit to cheating at some time in their academic careers

*http://education-portal.com/articles/75_to_98_Percent_of_College_Students_Have_Cheated.html

homework. Has that kind of thing ever happened to you? What's up with that?

My precious Bible tells me that after I repent and give my life to Christ, I receive the gift of the Holy Spirit—God himself, in spirit form, comes and indwells my body. I know, I know—you're picturing some kind of corny sci-fi movie where the body of some innocent farm boy is taken over by aliens. But it's true:

> *Or do you not know that your body is a temple of the Holy Spirit within you, whom you have from God? You are not your own...*
> (1 Corinthians 6:19).

Cool, right? So, what exactly does the Holy Spirit do within me? What kind of superhero powers do I get with God living inside me? Well, the Bible says this:

> *"And when he comes, he will convict the world concerning sin and righteousness and judgment"* (John 16:8).

In other words, the Holy Spirit tells us what is wrong (convict the world concerning sin), what is right (righteousness), and what the consequences are for both (judgment). So, if we are indwelled by the Holy Spirit and if we are able to know what is right and what is wrong, then why do we keep sinning? That's a brilliant beyond brilliant question! We keep sinning because our nature, even after salvation, is still sinful. So although we now have the Holy Spirit, we still have that sin nature (sometimes you hear it called "the flesh") that wants to sin.

To be honest, it's a battle—a battle that rages inside of us every day. And because God gives us the ability to choose, we often choose the way of our flesh, even when we know what is right. Here's how God explains it:

> [16] But I say, walk by the Spirit, and you will not gratify the desires of the flesh. [17] For the desires of the flesh are against the Spirit, and the desires of the Spirit are against the flesh, for these are opposed to each other, to keep you from doing the things you want to do (Galatians 5:16-17).

It's really easy to understand a battle. Maybe you have parents, family members, or friends who are soldiers. Or maybe some of you just love to play war video games on your game system. And if you can't relate to either of those, I'm sure you've seen battles in some of those great, epic movies— like The Lord of the Rings trilogy—that are terrifying. Well, if you think about it, there's a battle raging inside of you every minute of every day—a battle that you have the ability to win or lose. The only difference between this battle and the others is that YOU choose which side will win.

So when your parents ask you to tell the truth about something you would rather not, who is going to win, the Spirit or the flesh? When the girl sitting next to you at lunch is gossiping about something juicy, who is going to win, the Spirit or the flesh? When your friend offers to let you copy his new CD, who is going to win, the Spirit or the flesh? The choice is up to you. There is only one answer: You decide.

CHAPTER FOUR

COPYCAT

I remember that when I was a little kid, I adored my big brother and wanted to be just like him in absolutely every way. Literally! So, anything he did, I had to do, too. If he wanted to eat Cap'n Crunch® for breakfast, then I wanted to eat Cap'n Crunch® for breakfast.

If he told a funny joke, I had to tell a funny joke, too—usually the exact same one! If he wore a costume, I had to wear one, too. So if he was Peter Pan, then I was Peter Pan. Sure, I may have been wearing the Tinker Bell costume, but I was really Peter Pan on the inside.

As I grew older, I learned that there was a specific name for this kind of behavior: It's called being a "copycat," and it is often associated with a "baby" game played by two individuals, when one mirrors the other. Thankfully, I've grown up a little now and I've begun to leave some of my childhood games behind. Being a copycat was one I thought would disappear. Yes, I still love my brother, but I don't feel the need do every little thing he does anymore. However, I was wrong.

What I've learned is that we actually continue to play some of those "baby" games as we go throughout life, especially the copycat game.

Actually, God made us that way, and the Bible talks about this very thing. Check it out:

> ¹Therefore be imitators of God, as beloved children. ²And walk in love, as Christ loved us and gave himself up for us, a fragrant offering and sacrifice to God (Ephesians 5:1-2).

God knows that we like to copycat other people, and we are told to imitate God. And we have the very best example to follow: Jesus Christ. He lived as a human being, never sinned, and always pleased God the Father. It's amazing, really! So God says to imitate him. But sometimes it's hard to know exactly what Jesus would do in every situation, right? No kidding! This has been a problem for a lot of us as we are trying to please God in our lives but don't always know exactly what Jesus would do. But look at what Paul wrote to some Christians with the same problem:

> Be imitators of me, as I am of Christ (1 Corinthians 11:1).

Factoids about the church of Corinth
- Started by Paul
- A.D. 50
- In modern-day Greece
- Home of the temple of the Greek goddess Aphrodite
- Well known for sexual sinfulness

See, Paul was an older Christian. He knew a ton about living like Jesus, and that's why he told these Christians that if they weren't sure how to live like Jesus, they should watch and imitate him. In doing so, they would be imitating Jesus. These Christians had never seen Jesus before, but they knew

Paul and could watch how he lived, hear how he spoke, and see what he did.

Junior high is a pivotal time in a person's life. It sure was in mine! It's during these years that you lay the foundation for how you will build the rest of your life. The choices you make in junior high will set you up for the way you will live in high school. The choices you make in high school will set you up for the way you will live as an adult. Seems like a lot of pressure, doesn't it? Well, it kind of is, but you don't have to face it all alone.

My parents knew this little secret, so when I turned 13, they threw a huge surprise party for me—only it wasn't one of those cake-and-ice-cream kind of parties. Instead of inviting a bunch of my girlfriends with sleeping bags, my parents invited people who they knew would be my spiritual mentors in the upcoming years of my life. The guest  list featured a varied group of men and women from my church, my school, and my family's past, even friends who flew in from other states! All of these were strong Christian people who loved me. Everyone had prepared some Christ-centered advice for me and for my future. Some, who couldn't make the party in person, wrote me letters and others sent videos. It was a very special night, one I will never forget.

In the years since, these people have been my spiritual mentors—people in my own life, like Paul was to the people he lived with, whom I have looked to as an example. It's these people who have continually spoken words of truth, love, and encouragement to me. Some of them have even instructed and corrected me. Even though it was hard for me to hear what they sometimes had to say, I'm grateful for it.

> *Where there is no guidance, a people falls, but in an abundance of counselors there is safety* (Proverbs 11:14).

Now don't misunderstand me here. We are to follow Christ first and foremost. However, these are the men and women, along with my parents, that God has put in my life to imitate. In the crucial years that you are walking through right now, I encourage you to do the same. Find a person who lives like a Christian—or several people—whether that's your coach, or an older kid at school, or your youth pastor. Find someone who has already lived through the years that are coming up for you and has made good choices and has experienced success. Then act like this person. Be a copycat! Watch how this person lives. Listen to how this person talks. When you have a question about life, ask this person. And, when you're not sure what Jesus would do in a situation, think about what that person has done, and do the same thing.

But that's not the end of the "copycat" game. As much as you need to look to someone older to copy, you also need to be someone that another person can copy. My parents always put it this way:

> ## "Find older people to imitate and younger people to influence."

You see, we not only should find spiritual mentors, but we also should BE spiritual mentors to other people. Get involved in a younger person's life so he or she has a Christian example to follow, too. The challenge is on! Find older people in your life who love God (and love you) and imitate them.

Also, find a younger student in your life that you can influence for Christ—a younger student to whom you can speak words of truth, love, and encouragement. It will change that person's life, and it will change yours, too.

CHAPTER FIVE

BFF'S

Blessed is the man

who walks not in the counsel of the wicked,

nor stands in the way of sinners,

nor sits in the seat of scoffers;

but his delight is in the law of the Lord,

and on his law he meditates day and night

(Psalm 1:1-2).

Friends are a fundamental part of our growth and development, especially our spiritual growth. When I started middle school, I had no idea of the changes that were about to take place in my life physically, emotionally, and spiritually.

It was August of 2007, the first day of sixth grade. Of course, I got sick and had to miss the whole first week of school. So there I was, just a chubby little kid coming in a week later than everyone else. I didn't know where I was going but everyone else did, I took the wrong binder to some classes, and I even got scolded for eating in the hallway (twice)—but other than that, it was great! Finally, after all the long years of waiting down in elementary school, with no freedom, no authority, and absolutely no choice in the cafeteria, I had arrived!

Middle school. A world filled with endless opportunities! I even had what all the older kids talked about: a locker! In my mind, I just didn't know how it could get any better than that! Looking back on it, it would have been nice if I actually could have opened the locker, but just having one made all the difference. For the first time in my entire schooling career, I didn't have to walk down the hall with my classmates in a single-file line. I finally had the independence to walk how I wanted to walk, and as you can probably imagine, that's a big deal for an 11-year-old!

I wasn't the only person who had that independence. Every student had it, and in a strange, unspoken way, every student was going to have to choose not only how to walk down the hall, but choose which hall in life they were going to travel.

Middle school is where students begin to choose a distinct path. Most choose darkness. Its hall is wide and easy to walk in, full of the "cool" kids, and accepting of your natural, sinful behaviors. However, a select few choose the light. Its hall is not as easy to walk down. Nothing new here; in Matthew 7, Jesus talks about these same two paths:

> ^{13}"Enter by the narrow gate. For the gate is wide and the way is easy that leads to destruction, and those who enter by it are many. ^{14}For the gate is narrow and the way is hard that leads to life, and those who find it are few" (Matthew 7:13-14).

Not very encouraging for the masses, is it? Jesus says that the path to life is narrow and very few find it. But for those of us on the narrow path, choosing friends becomes extremely important. As the verse at the beginning of this chapter says, you will be blessed if you avoid bad friendships. Instead, you must find friends that are infatuated with the Word of God and sold out for Christ, just like you are. You may find five like that or you may just find one, but the cool thing is, the numbers don't matter. The only thing that matters is that the ones you seek are serious about being Christians. I hear it all the time from my dad. He says this:

"Show me your friends and I'll show you your future."

You know what? He is so right! When I think back to middle school, I realize none of my friends were perfect, they weren't "spiritual giants," but all of them focused on the Word of God. I always knew that my best friend, Ellie, was someone who loved me, prayed for me, encouraged me to grow closer to Christ, and stood by me even when the going got tough.

And I did the same for her. When I think of her, I think of a verse in Proverbs:

> *Iron sharpens iron, and one man sharpens another* (Proverbs 27:17).

Admittedly, it's easy to choose friends based on who is popular, who is on your sports team, who is funny, who is beautiful, or who is just plain convenient! And I'm not saying that you shouldn't have any friends at all that aren't Christians. However, if you pick your closest friends, your BFF's, based on factors such as these, you can never guarantee that they will share your values and be like-minded with you when it comes to the Word of God.

I won't lie to you: Finding good friends isn't always easy. Sometimes you have to let go of friends you like because they hurt your relationship with God, sometimes you have to look for unexpected friendships with people that you wouldn't have thought would be your pals, and sometimes you have to be willing to be friendless for a while. But it's crucial that you do because you become what your friends are, good or bad. And if they're bad?

> *Do not be deceived: "Bad company ruins good morals"* (1 Corinthians 15:33).

Above anything else you do, choose the narrow way to life and surround yourself with other people that have done the same. It may be the harder hall to walk down, but you'll never regret it.

CHAPTER SIX

IN vs. OF

I absolutely love how God's Word is just as relevant to my life today as it was to someone living a thousand years ago. It just goes to show that although architecture, fashion, technology, and music change, people are pretty much the same from age to age. I'm super aware of this when I start to study history—or when my own parents tell me about when they were in high school. Sure, the clothes definitely look different, but the people are just like the ones I know! I'm infatuated with God's words because God made us, so when he says something, I trust that it's what I need.

One of the things the Bible tells us is that we are strangers in this world (see Psalm 119:19). And although we live here on earth, we don't belong here, and we are not like everybody else. I'm friends with Michael Tait, one of the original members of DC Talk, who sang the famous song "Jesus Freak." (He's a fun guy, by the way.) In that song, we are called to be a "freak" for Jesus. Well, I believe God wants us to take it even one step further. I believe that we are called not only to be a "freak" FOR Jesus, but we also are called to be a "freak" FROM the world! If we are

> "Jesus Freak" video:
> http://www.youtube.com/
> watch?v=2jDnVpCNlyY

Christians, we are to be like Christ, and being like Christ means that the things we say, do, and think are going to be radically different, even "freakish," from the things most people in the world say, do, and think. God says this:

> *14 As obedient children, do not be conformed to the passions of your former ignorance, 15 but as he who called you is holy, you also be holy in all your conduct, 16 since it is written, "You shall be holy, for I am holy"* (I Peter 1:14-16).

Holy: set aside as pure for God

Be holy. Now, that's radical! Not "Be good" or "Try hard" or "Blend in," but "Be holy." So, how do we do that?

> *Do not be conformed to this world, but be transformed by the renewal of your mind, that by testing you may discern what is the will of God, what is good and acceptable and perfect* (Romans 12:2).

Just living in the world makes us susceptible to becoming like the world, sometimes without even realizing it, and what we forget is that the things of the world—the celebrities, fashions, and fads—constantly change. As soon as you "get" how to be "cool," the standards for "cool" change! What's with that?

On the other hand, the things of God never change. Never. That's why God calls us to resist being like the world by changing (renewal) our thinking (mind). God asks us to be infatuated with spiritual things, the things that will last forever, and not the things of this earth that are meaningless and will pass away.

Read this:

> ¹If then you have been raised with Christ, seek the things that are above, where Christ is, seated at the right hand of God. ²Set your minds on things that are above, not on things that are on earth (Colossians 3:1-2).

So let's get down to business here, OK? What exactly do I mean when I suggest that we are to be "holy" and not to live like the world? Well, some ways are probably pretty obvious, right? We are not to lie. We are not to steal. We are not to kill people. All right, we can all agree on that stuff, and maybe you don't do any of those things already. But how about when I ask you about some things you may love—like your friends, your music, the television shows, or the movies you watch. Yikes! It's maybe a little harder now.

Really think about it. Are those things "holy"? Do those things cause you to love God more or love the world more? Do those things make you look more like God or more like the way everybody else at your school or in your community looks? Are you trying to be like Christ or like the people who are acting in those movies or singing those songs?

You may be saying, "Not everything in the world is bad, is it? How can I tell which things are good and which ones aren't?" I'm glad you asked. See, God doesn't spell out too many "do's" and "don'ts" for us. God really isn't into a bunch of rules that we have to memorize, but God does give us some common-sense truths that we can apply to our own individual circumstances. Here's one of those truths:

> *Finally, brothers, whatever is true, whatever is honorable, whatever is just, whatever is pure, whatever is lovely, whatever is commendable, if there is any excellence, if there is anything worthy of praise, think about these things* (Philippians 4:8).

There. That sounds pretty simple, but now you actually have to apply it to your life. So when you are evaluating that television show you enjoy watching, ask yourself if it has any of the qualities listed in this verse. If it doesn't, then don't watch it. Guard your eyes! When you are thinking about that band you enjoy listening to, ask yourself if it has any of the qualities listed in this verse. If it doesn't, then don't listen to it. Guard your ears! When you are thinking about those friends you hang out with, ask yourself if they have any of the qualities listed in this verse. If they don't, then don't hang out with them. Guard your heart!

Maybe you've never thought about things from this perspective. You may know that some of the things you enjoy are not holy, but you think you can "handle it." But can you, really? These things will tremendously influence you, whether you admit it or not. You will get used to them, you will make excuses for them, and, in time, you will even grow to love them. At that point, they will be incredibly painful to remove from your life, and you may never do it.

THINGS I SHOULD GIVE UP

_____

_____

_____

_____

_____

_____

_____

_____

_____

_____

_____

I suppose it's kind of like a filter. We use different kinds of filters for all kinds of things. Think about a water filter. Have you ever used one? A water filter is used when you want to purify regular water. Lots of us use water filters every day at home. We take the regular tap water and run it through our filter to make it clean and pure and much healthier for us to drink.

Well, if you think about it, we can use the Word of God as a filter in our lives. We can take the things of this world and pour them through the filter of God's Word. Let the filter catch the things that do not meet God's standard. Then choose to throw those things away, because they are not healthy for you. What passes through the filter is great to enjoy—and trust me: This world is FULL of great, enjoyable things that glorify a holy God!

This past summer, a friend gave me a bracelet to help me as I ask myself what is OK to enjoy and what is not. On it, there are three simple words I can ask myself before I decide: "Is It Holy?" You see, some things are good. Some things I enjoy. Some things may not be very good, but I can handle them. Some things may be fine.

THINGS I AM FREE TO ENJOY

————————————

————————————

————————————

————————————

————————————

————————————

————————————

————————————

————————————

————————————

————————————

————————————

But when I ask myself, "Is it holy?" that changes everything. Holiness means being set aside and pure for God. So is your friendship pure for God? Is that movie pure for God? Are those lyrics pure for God? It's something to think about.

So, whether you eat or drink, or whatever you do, do all to the glory of God" (1 Corinthians 10:31).

CHAPTER SEVEN

OMG...
It's a big deal

"You shall not take the name of the Lord your God in vain, for the Lord will not hold him guiltless who takes his name in vain"

(Exodus 20:7).

Life is filled with change, and with every major change, a new season of life begins. One big change in life arrives when we start high school. When I was getting ready to start high school, I kept hearing people refer to the high school years as the "glory days" or the "best years of your life." Those people are lame! Living life for God's glory at any age is so much better than anything your four high school years have to offer!

In my case, high school has been, in some ways, the opposite of what people predicted. To be completely honest with you, the start of high school was kind of a disaster for me: The building was strange, the kids were huge, the hallways were loud, and most of the teachers didn't know my name. You need to understand that I'm a pretty strong girl, but even I was intimidated. It was a big adjustment because it was all so different from the comforts I had enjoyed in my sweet, happy, cozy middle school years.

I was freshman class president, and I thought that out of anyone in my grade, I should be the one to have high school all figured out, right? But I found out that those first few days were pretty scary, and I hate to admit it, but I had quite a few tear-filled nights. But do not dismay my dear reader! High school didn't remain grim forever! As the days and months went by, things began to slowly get better. I started to get used to the building, and either I grew a little taller or I just got used to the bigger kids.

However, there was one big change in high school that I just wasn't going to ever "get used to," and that was how the students at my Christian school showed zero respect in the way they chose to use the Lord's name. I could hardly walk down the hall without hearing half a dozen kids say, "Oh my God!" It's not like they were even trying to hide it! They didn't even notice they were saying it, and it hurt. Every time I heard it, it hurt. I knew this was wrong, but what could I do about it? I mean, what would people think of me if I spoke up, and what difference would it make anyway?

None, right?

Around Christmastime, everything changed. The school dean had called for an end-of-semester student government meeting. It was held bright and early, before school started. I'm usually useless at an hour this ridiculously early in the morning, but this morning was different. For some reason, I was wide-awake. Little did I know the way God planned on using me!

The dean asked the student government officers, "Now that you have observed for a semester, what are some improvements you think we can make in our school?" Immediately, a needed "improvement" came to my mind: the swearing issue, the fact that most of the students, who claim to be Christians, misuse God's name! Here was my chance to discuss the biggest issue my school has, right? Finally! Instinctively I went to speak up, but when I opened my mouth to talk, I realized another girl had already begun her answer.

Leaning back in my chair, I sighed, biding my time while this girl blabbered on about recycling (of all things...) and keeping our hallways clean. How long was I going to have to wait to discuss what was REALLY important? On and on she droned, until finally I decided I'd had enough. It was now or never. "I know something we need to change!" I blurted. With that, every head spun around and fixed their gaze on me. There was a sudden silence, as even Gina-go-green had shut up to stare me down. I swallowed hard and began to pour out my heart.

The meeting ended with no one offering a resolution to the problem, but I couldn't stop thinking about it. I kept thinking, "I know this is problem, but what can I do to change anything?" So I asked one of my spiritual mentors: my mother. We discussed the whole situation, and I asked her how I could make the kids stop doing that. She said, "Jacqueline, you can't control what other people do.

Actually, no one can. But you CAN control what YOU do." And that's when we devised a plan.

Three weeks later, right after Christmas break, I was standing on a stage in front of the entire high school. I had printed a large poster. It was pretty simple. At the bottom was God's commandment from Exodus 20. At the top was the statement: I will not say "Oh my God." I explained my conviction to the whole student body. I read them God's words and then I told them that although I couldn't control what they chose to say, I could control what I chose to say and was making a pledge to NOT misuse the Lord's name. I showed them the poster, I signed it in front of them, and I asked them to join me. Students who agreed with it could sign their names on it.

For the rest of the year, that poster hung in the front hallway of my school. Most of the students didn't sign it, but some of them did.

"I will not say 'Oh my God'"

"YOU SHALL NOT TAKE THE NAME OF THE LORD YOUR GOD IN VAIN, FOR THE LORD WILL NOT LEAVE HIM UNPUNISHED WHO TAKES HIS NAME IN VAIN."

Either way, I know a lot of them had to think about their vocabulary, and I know that God was glorified.

I'm not telling you this story to make me look super spiritual. I'm telling you this story because this problem, taking God's name in vain, is a problem that isn't unique to my little school. It's everywhere and it's a big deal. The culture we live in today says, "Oh my God," or "OMG" all the time. It's at school, it's in magazines, and sometimes I even hear adults say it at Christian functions! Our society uses that phrase so much, that I can hardly go see a movie where I don't hear the name of God misused by every single actor.

It breaks my heart, because I know this is wrong. The first time the Word of God was written down, God wrote it himself, with his very own finger (see Exodus 31:18). Did you know that? God was writing the Ten Commandments, basic laws God wanted people to obey. I find it shockingly amazing how concise God was. God basically summed up right living in only 10 points, 10 rules. There are tons of rules in basketball, chess, or even driving a car, and we seem to follow them easily, so why is it so hard to follow 10 rules that an Almighty God gave us?

Rule number three: "Do NOT take the name of God in vain." Saying "Oh my God" is taking the name of God in vain, and so is the acronym "OMG." It's a big deal! If it weren't such a big deal, God wouldn't have written it himself as one of the Ten Commandments.

Look, what you say is super important and what you talk about matters to God. What do you say without even realizing it? What do you talk about? Is it stupid or inappropriate? This isn't a new

The Ten Commandments

1. You shall have no other gods before me.
2. You shall not make for yourself an image in the form of anything in heaven above or on the earth beneath or in the waters below.
3. You shall not misuse the name of the LORD your God, for the Lord will not hold anyone guiltless who misuses his name.
4. Remember the Sabbath day by keeping it holy.
5. Honor your father and your mother, so that you may live long in the land the LORD your God is giving you.
6. You shall not murder.
7. You shall not commit adultery.
8. You shall not steal.
9. You shall not give false testimony against your neighbor.
10. You shall not covet your neighbor's house. You shall not covet your neighbor's wife, or his male or female servant, his ox or donkey, or anything that belongs to your neighbor.

problem. Through the Apostle Paul, God writes to us again about this very thing, giving us pretty clear instruction:

> Let there be no filthiness nor foolish talk nor crude joking, which are out of place, but instead let there be thanksgiving (Ephesians 5:4).

If we are followers of Christ, we need to SOUND different from those who do not know the words of God. What we say matters to God, to other followers of Christ, and to the people watching us who do not know Christ. I pledge to be a person who is reverent and respectful of the Lord's name in response to all God has done for me. Will you join me?

CHAPTER EIGHT

PARENTS MATTER

Some birthdays are just more significant than others, don't you think? Like your first birthday. Too bad none of us remember that one. Another is when you turn 10. Finally, you're in "double digits!" How about when you turn 13? Suddenly, a new maturity descends upon you, overnight, as you reach the pinnacle of life and you're finally a TEENAGER. (OK, not much really changes from being 12, but it's still exciting!) Someone's "Sweet 16" is another one of these important birthdays, especially in the South, where I come from—it's a REALLY big deal. This birthday is always celebrated, and sometimes people even throw huge parties: formal dances, costume parties, themed events, professional photographers—the works!

For me, it's that time of life when many of my friends are turning 16. In fact, recently I had the privilege of throwing a custom-designed "Sweet 16" birthday party for my friend Adam. I had some fabulous ideas, and I knew I had to start planning early. One way I got creative was with the guest list. I didn't want it to be the typical party, all kids from school,

from the same grade. So I invited a whole variety of people, including pastors at my church, small group leaders, both older and younger friends from school, and members of his extended family—everyone I could think of that he would enjoy, from grandparents in their 70s all the way down to a little baby who was less than a year old.

Another way I got creative was making a video that I planned to show while we served the birthday cake. The video was unique because I filmed, ahead of time, every party guest answering questions. Some of the questions were just for fun, while other ones were related specifically to the party theme, but one went deeper. I asked the guests to give their advice on "surviving 16." I found their responses fascinating, because practically every adult's answer was the same. They all basically said this: I know it's not always easy, but if you honor your father and mother, it will go well for you.

This got me thinking. I have such a good relationship with my parents that making an effort to "honor" them never really crossed my mind. But as I listened to the advice, given over and over by one person after the next, I realized something: They were right! It wasn't some mistake that God gave us parents and wants us to listen to them, honor them, and obey them:

'Children, obey your parents in the Lord, for this is right. ²"Honor your father and mother" (this is the first commandment with a promise), ³"that it may go well with you and that you may live long in the land" (Ephesians 6:1-3).

Your parents matter! I'm not just saying that as some cute cliché. I truly mean it. I realize I may only be a couple of years older than you are, but I've had to walk down some roads you are about to walk down, and I want you to consider my advice. Parents are older and wiser, and almost all want the best for their kids. They are the only people in the whole world that will love you, no matter what!

Additionally, they were teenagers once, and believe it or not, they have felt the same things you are feeling. They have made both good choices and bad ones, and they can teach you things so that you don't have to make the same mistakes. They're further down the road of life, and remarkably, the roads we travel remain similar to the roads they faced at our age.

Obviously, listening to and obeying your parents isn't a concept that my party guests were the first to suggest. They knew it was good advice that God gives us in the Bible. These were people who are infatuated with God's Word, too!

More advice on the video:
- Don't stay out after midnight. Nothing good happens after midnight
- Don't drive too fast
- Surround yourself with other godly men and women
- Ask a lot of questions
- Only choose friends that love the Lord

WARNING: While the Bible teaches us to respect our parents, following their lead while they're sinning or asking you to sin is especially difficult. If you find yourself in this situation, I'd recommend you sit down with a trusted youth pastor, small group leader, or adult to help you navigate this difficult situation.

Look at this:

> [8] *Hear, my son, your father's instruction,*
> *and forsake not your mother's teaching,*
> [9] *for they are a graceful garland for your head*
> *and pendants for your neck* (Proverbs 1:8-9).

The first part of this verse is saying to listen to and act upon parental advice. The second part is saying that if you do that, it will go well for you. Did you catch that? It's the very same advice all of those people gave in my friend's video! That's because God's words work. They're true, and they guide us to success if we listen and obey them. Honoring our parents is huge!

> "Honor your father and your mother, that your days may be long in the land that the Lord your God is giving you" (Exodus 20:12).

Even if your parents are not Christians, I believe God still wants you to honor them. Notice that God doesn't say, "Honor only your Christian father and only your Christian mother." It says to honor your father and mother, period. I don't know all the details of your circumstance or family situation, but I do believe God has handpicked our parents for a specific reason and to complete a specific purpose in our lives. The God who created the universe has chosen the people he wants to raise us. I feel like a celebrity! Why would anyone not let the parents God picked for them be a part of their lives, their friends, their conversations, their feelings, their heart, or their walk with God?

Please hear me: I am all for spiritual mentors outside your family, but if your parents are grounded in God's Word and are faithfully walking in the truth, I believe, hands down, that they should be the biggest advisers in your life and that their advice should always come before that of a spiritual mentor. We pick our spiritual mentors, but God has picked our parents.

No matter how old we are or who our parents are, God's Word instructs us to honor our parents, because parents matter.

CHAPTER NINE

THE TWO-FACED COIN

Aren't computers great? I would hate to live without mine! I watch ridiculous YouTube® videos on it, I listen to music on it, I store and edit photos on it, I make movies on it, I even use it for less exciting things—like schoolwork, such as looking at math tutorials (oh, joy!) and researching all kinds of interesting, and some not-so-interesting, stuff. But if there is anything that has thoroughly consumed our generation's computer use, it's social networking. It's an amazing concept, really. With just a click of a mouse, you can catch up on all of your "friends" and know every intimate detail about their personal, private lives.

Facebook® statistics*:
- Founded in February 2004
- More than 800 million active users
- More than 50 percent of users log on in any given day
- Average user has 130 friends
- Average user is connected to 80 community pages, groups, and events
- More than 250 million photos are uploaded every day
- More than 70 languages available on the site
- More than 75 percent of users are outside the U.S.
- More than 7 million apps and websites are integrated with Facebook

* http://www.facebook.com/press/info.php?statistics

Many of my friends have created profiles on Facebook. I realize every user is different, but my friends with Facebook accounts seem completely addicted to this social networking site, checking in multiple times a day for status updates or to see what other people have posted. And my friends are not all that unique. Did you know that if you are an average user, you are spending eight hours a month[3] updating your status or seeing what your "friends" have to say about their school, friends, teachers, sports teams, or whatever else has them captivated at that miniscule moment? Another statistic says that the average user is spending more time on Facebook than they are on Yahoo®, Google®, Microsoft®, YouTube®, Wikipedia®, and Amazon® combined[4]. Wow!

No matter what views you hold on Facebook or other social networking sites, it's easy to say that with a total of 2 billion posts and 250 million photos uploaded every day[5], the 800 million members prove that Facebook has become an obsession with a tremendous impact on our society. I mean, 800 million users? Seriously? That's like everyone AND their grandmas. Crazy!

So what's my point? Why all the Facebook statistics? (WARNING: You might want to "unfriend" me right now, because what I'm about to tell you will show that, personally, I'm not Facebook's biggest fan.) Well, it's because of this: I believe that social networking sites like Facebook are not only an addictive waste of your time, but that they also regularly lead to sin: that sneaky little sin of comparison.

You see, whenever you compare yourself to someone else, there are only two possible conclusions: (1) You realize you are "better" than the other person and you become prideful or (2) you realize that the other person is "better" and you become envious. Really, the sin of comparison is best described as a two-faced coin. On one side, it is the snooty face of pride, and on the other, the greedy face of envy.

So how does this relate to using social networking sites? Well, on one side of the coin, everyday millions people are living their lives for the purpose of posting it online. Think about it. How many times have you heard someone say, "Can you take a picture of me? I want to post it online." My question is always the same: Why? Why do you want hundreds of people to see hundreds of photos of where you're vacationing, what your new outfit looks like, the people you are with, and what you are doing? I've debated the question over and over, and at the end of the day, I've concluded that it's just pride. Chances are, you want others to see what you're doing with your life and to convince them that it's better than what they're doing with theirs.

On the other side of the coin, millions of teenagers spend their lives constantly on the Internet, relentlessly scanning through people's updates to carefully analyze every little detail of a particular photo or post from some guy or girl from school, half of whom they never even speak to face to face. Really? And how do you think they usually end up feeling when they see how others live their lives? Upset. Hurt. Envious.

But the Word of God calls us to something totally different.
It says this:

> *25 If we live by the Spirit, let us also walk by the Spirit. 26 Let us not become conceited, provoking one another, envying one another* (Galatians 5:25-26).

I know that the Word of God convicts the heart of his children. And so it doesn't really matter what I have to say, only what God says. And here, he tells us not to become conceited or proud or envious. In fact, God really wants us to be in the middle of those two; he wants us to be content. Here's what Paul wrote:

> *11 Not that I am speaking of being in need, for I have learned in whatever situation I am to be content. 12 I know how to be brought low, and I know how to abound. In any and every circumstance, I have learned the secret of facing plenty and hunger, abundance and need* (Philippians 4:11-12).

Now, I'm not arguing that the Bible says it's a sin to use social networking sites, but all over God's Word, we read that we are to be content with what we have, and if we cannot be content with what we have, we are sinning.

Content. Happy. Satisfied.

Can you be on Facebook and be content? When you see that your classmate has the brand-new boots your mom says you can't afford, can you be content? When you see that the girl you like was at the movies with another boy, can you be content?

The bottom line is, God doesn't want us to be infatuated with our own lives or anyone else's life. God wants us to be infatuated with him, his work, and his words! When all that we know is gone, God will still be. He has always been. He is God! Think about that for a moment: God is the only thing that is truly worth "checking in" on, and his "posts" are the only ones worth reading. We need to be content with just belonging to God.

Keep your life free from love of money, and be content with what you have, for he has said, "I will never leave you nor forsake you" (Hebrews 13:5).

CHAPTER TEN

ARE YOU GOING TO ANSWER THAT CALL?

Have you ever read 1 Samuel 3? Take a few minutes and check it out right now. It's an amazing story. Awakened in the middle of the night, Samuel received his call from God, a call that would alter the way he would live from that day forward, a call that would last a lifetime. Amazingly, God had to call out to Samuel three times before he figured out who was speaking! But Samuel finally got it and listened.

God calls people to all sorts of things: big things, small things, and even some things that seem impossible. The call is one thing, but how we respond is another. In 1 Samuel, God clearly called Samuel, and Samuel responded by saying this:

"Speak, for your servant hears" (1 Samuel 3:10).

Facts about Samuel
- Son of Hannah and Elkanah
- Samuel means either "Heard of God" or "Heard has God"
- Around 3 years old, Samuel was given to God to serve Eli in the tabernacle
- Never cut his hair
- Anointed first two kings of Israel
- Judge and military leader

I think it's so cool how God filled the Bible with the accounts of real-life people to learn from because they are not too different from us. God called to Samuel to do things, and God is going to call you to do things in your life, too. Some things may be easy and others may be hard. Your job is pretty simple: It's to recognize God's voice and respond to God's call.

Admittedly, it can be difficult to recognize God's voice amidst the many other influences in our lives. Although I have never personally heard the audible voice of God, I have undoubtedly experienced God's call, through the stirring of my spirit, to a few specific things in my life. The key, of course, is discerning between God's prompting and something else, even my own good intentions, when that "stirring" occurs.

But how do we know when it is God calling, if we can't audibly hear God's voice? To begin with, and most importantly, God's call never contradicts the truths of Scripture. God will never call you to do something that goes against what the Bible clearly teaches. You see, the Word of God contains everything God knows we need to lead a successful life.

"This Book of the Law shall not depart from your mouth, but you shall meditate on it day and night, so that you may be careful to do according to all that is written in it. For then you will make your way prosperous, and then you will have good success" (Joshua 1:8).

It is easy to fall into the trap of believing that my feelings or my good ideas or my friends' suggestions are really the calling of God. However, we must remember that our feelings change, our ideas are unreliable, and our friends may not know what they're talking about! So, when trying to recognize God's voice, we must base our decisions off of something unchanging: God's undefeatable, holy Word.

On to the second part: responding to God's call. I loved my junior high years. They rocked! During this time I made great strides in my walk with the Lord. I had many Christ-like mentors during that time of my life who had a huge influence on the decisions I made. Because of this, once I graduated to high school, I really felt God was calling me to do something with junior high students, something that could help guide them along that crazy road. I sensed that God wanted me to be a mentor, just as I had been mentored. I knew I was to respond to God's call in my life. So I contacted my youth pastor and asked if I could work as a small group leader for the junior high youth group at my church.

WHAT'S GOD CALLING YOU TO DO?

_____

_____

_____

_____

_____

_____

_____

Now, I'm a big Duke University basketball fan, and one night the youth group happened to land during ESPN's Rival Week. Ugh, the conflict! Well, I chose to go to church, and after youth group I could've rushed home quickly to watch the games. However, I felt God was calling me to talk to one of the girls in my small group. I followed the call and moments later I had the privilege of leading one of my students to faith in Christ.

Will you follow God's call? Every Christian, no matter how young or old in their faith, has been given a talent or a special ability from God. He gives us a unique gift so we will use it to be his hands and his feet in our world. You may know your gift; it's probably something you know you are good at and enjoy. Well then, use it! Use the talents God has given you as he calls you to do things in life.

> *Let no one despise you for your youth, but set the believers an example in speech, in conduct, in love, in faith, in purity* (1 Timothy 4:12).

Will you strive to be like Timothy and not let anyone look down on you because you are young, but obediently respond to the call of God on your life? I hope you will answer the call!

WHAT ARE YOUR GIFTS?

_____   _____

_____   _____

_____   _____

_____   _____

CHAPTER ELEVEN

BECOMING INFATUATED

Perhaps, after reading this whole book, you've begun to be infatuated with the Word of God yourself. Praise the Lord! That's awesome. But now you are probably asking, "How do I read and understand something so big and so complicated as the Bible?" You may be surprised to find out it's not nearly as hard as you think because the Bible was written for us to understand, even as teenagers. God didn't make it some big mystery that we need someone to explain to us. Start by getting a good translation, like the New International Version (NIV) or the New American Standard Bible (NASB), and then just read it like you would read any other message someone would write to you.

> Do your best to present yourself to God as one approved, a worker who has no need to be ashamed, rightly handling the word of truth (2 Timothy 2:15).

In an attempt to "correctly handle" the Bible, let me recommend a few study methods that have really helped me:

First, before you begin to read the Bible, pray. Pray that the Holy Spirit will help you understand what you are reading and that the Spirit will direct your thoughts. This is super important because it is during your reading that the Spirit will really convict your heart of things.

Second, as you are reading the Bible, the Spirit may make certain words or sentences stand out to you; it could be something God is convicting you to do or to avoid. Highlight or underline these sections. There is a reason the Spirit is emphasizing these words for you. Mark it and make notes in the margins. It will really help you remember what you are learning and assist you in finding it again, when you want to.

Third, when you read the Bible, don't just read one verse; read a whole paragraph or two—what I would call a "passage." Sometimes, people suggest you read a verse that is really meaningful to them. But if you only read that one, single verse, you will often miss the big picture. It is always best to back up and read four or five verses before that verse and then move forward

> "But the Helper, the Holy Spirit, whom the Father will send in my name, he will teach you all things and bring to your remembrance all that I have said to you" (John 14:26).

> "When the Spirit of truth comes, he will guide you into all the truth, for he will not speak on his own authority, but whatever he hears he will speak, and he will declare to you the things that are to come" (John 16:13).

> The sum of Your word is truth, And every one of Your righteous ordinances is everlasting (Psalm 119:160 NASB).

> All your words are true; all your righteous laws are eternal (Psalm 119:160 NIV).

four or five verses after the verse, to really understand what is being said. This is reading a whole passage, from the start of the thought to the end of the thought.

Fourth, read the same passage for a couple of days. The best way for the words of God to be understood is to read the verses several times before moving on. Haven't you heard that before? I think my math teacher just told me that same thing today—we do the same math problems over and over to be sure we really have it, right? So read the same verses for two or three days before you move on to the next passage.

Finally, start one book of the Bible and don't move on until you finish the book. The best way to really understand what is being said in a book is to read the whole thing. So pick a book of the Bible to read, and read it all before you move to another book, even if that means you are reading one book, like James, for a long time. You would never read just one scene in a Shakespeare play or one chapter in a novel and walk away thinking you knew what the story was about, would you? I doubt it. So if you read a whole book in the Bible, by the time you are finished, you are really going to know what that book is talking about.

> [6] "And these words that I command you today shall be on your heart. [7] You shall teach them diligently to your children, and shall talk of them when you sit in your house, and when you walk by the way, and when you lie down, and when you rise. [8] You shall bind them as a sign on your hand, and they shall be as frontlets between your eyes. [9] You shall write them on the doorposts of your house and on your gates" (Deuteronomy 6:6-9).

So, to recap:

Pray before you begin.

Highlight words that stick out.

Read a passage, not just a verse.

Read the same passage for a few days.

Read the whole book before you move on.

This is a great starting point, so get at it! May this be the continuation or the very beginning of your own love affair with God and God's precious Word. May this become your life's addiction. May it obsess you, as it has thousands and thousands before you. And may God be glorified through you as you apply what you learn to your life. I trust that you, too, will become totally infatuated.

[7]The law of the Lord is perfect,

reviving the soul;

the testimony of the Lord is sure,

making wise the simple;

[8]the precepts of the Lord are right,

rejoicing the heart;

the commandment of the Lord is pure,

enlightening the eyes;

[9]the fear of the Lord is clean,

enduring forever;

the rules of the Lord are true,

and righteous altogether.

[10]More to be desired are they than gold,

even much fine gold;

sweeter also than honey

and drippings of the honeycomb.

[11]Moreover, by them is your servant warned;

in keeping them there is great reward

(Psalm 19:7-11).

ENDNOTES

1. sciencedaily.com/releases/2010/10/101022184957.htm

2. articles.cnn.com/2007-02-14/health/love.science_1_scans-caudate-amygdala?_s=PM:HEALTH

3. facebook.com/press/info.php?statistics

4. theatlantic.com/business/archive/2010/02/facebook-google-yahoo-microsoft-wikipedia/36089/

5. facebook.com/press/info.php?statistics